CLAIRE

BOUNCE

Illustrations by Angela Mitson Written by Giles Reed

PUBLISHED BY STUDIO PUBLICATIONS (IPSWICH) LIMITED
32 PRINCES STREET, IPSWICH, SUFFOLK, ENGLAND

Bounce is one of the Munch Bunch.

Bounce is a Spring Onion and is very clever at making things.

He made the tub that stands in his garden and he made the front door on his green bottle home.

One windy day, Bounce decided to make a kite.

He borrowed some scissors from Lizzie Leek, some sticks, a pot of glue and a ball of string from Tom Tomato, and some old bow-ties from Adam Avocado.

As soon as he had finished making the kite, he decided to go to the park to try it out.

Spud and Tom Tomato were already there.

"Gosh, that is a big kite, Bounce," said Spud. "Did you make it yourself?"

"Of course I did," replied Bounce.

"May we watch you fly it?" asked Tom.

"You can help me if you like," said Bounce.

So Tom and Spud held the kite while Bounce walked backwards, gradually letting out more string as he went.

He reached the top of the hill and yelled out, "OK, Tom, let it go now!"

Tom and Spud let go of the kite, and it flew into the air.

Spud and Tom watched as the kite climbed higher and higher.

Suddenly, a huge gust of wind caught the kite.

Before Bounce could do anything, he found himself sailing through the air holding on to the string.

“HELP!” cried Bounce.

But it was too late. Spud and Tom were a long way below him.

The kite rose up and up, carrying Bounce higher and higher.

Very soon Spud and Tom were just two tiny dots on the ground.

Up and up went the kite, until Bounce found himself high above the clouds.

"Brr," he chattered. "It's very cold up here."

Suddenly a yellow aeroplane appeared out of nowhere.

At first Bounce was very frightened. Then he wondered whether the pilot could rescue him.

But the aeroplane zoomed off again into the distance.

The kite continued on its journey.

"Oh I do wish I could get back to the ground," said Bounce. "I'm ever so scared!"

"We'll get you down," said a small voice.

And suddenly five blackbirds appeared and started pecking at the kite.

Gradually a hole was made in the kite by the blackbirds.

The hole became so big that the kite fell in half and Bounce started to fall to the ground.

"Help!" he cried.

Down, down, down Bounce fell until suddenly he stopped.

He had fallen into the middle of a tree.

The string from the kite was tied all round the branches but Bounce still held on.

When Tom and Spud arrived, all they could see were Bounce's legs sticking out from the tree.

"We came as fast as we could," panted Spud.

"Are you all right?" asked Tom. "Yes, thank you, but please get me out of this tree," pleaded Bounce.

“Oh thank you,” said Bounce when his feet finally touched the ground. “That was very frightening. I didn’t think I would ever get down again.

“Your kite is ruined,” said Spud.

“Never mind,” said Bounce, “let’s go home and I’ll make a better one.”

Tom and Spud watched eagerly as Bounce set to work again.

It didn't take long for him to finish making another kite.

"Let's go and fly it in the park," said Bounce.

"What a super idea," said Tom and Spud together.

The kite flew even better than the first one.

But this time Bounce didn't go flying with it.

Do you know why?

Because Bounce had put some heavy weights in his boots to keep him on the ground!

Acknowledgement: This story of Bounce was adapted by Giles Reed, from an original idea by Jim Raff.